How To Not Be a People Pleaser

The Ultimate Guide on How to Stop Being a People Pleaser

John Annabel

Table of Contents

Chapter 1

Understanding People Pleasing

A people-pleaser is exactly what it sounds like; someone who is constantly trying to please others. Even if it means they don't have time for themselves.

People-pleasing is not a recognized mental health disorder. However, it is a mental health condition that many people today suffer from, and it frequently leads to emotional and mental health issues.

Many people-pleasers are compassionate individuals with a high level of empathy. However, the issue for people-pleasers goes beyond simply wanting to be kind and considerate.

Low self-esteem is a significant motivator for someone who is a people-pleaser. Esteem is derived from the Latin aestimare, which means "to estimate," so self-esteem simply refers to how you value yourself.

The majority of people who have low self-esteem grew up in homes where they were not truly valued. They did not feel validated or loved for whatever reason, which could include neglect or abuse.

So their constant enthusiasm and need to please others stems from their low self-esteem. They believe that by saying yes to everything and everyone, they will prove that they are valuable and loved.

From pleasing parents to pleasing others

People-pleasing frequently begins in childhood when the child learns to be a parent-pleaser. To satisfy their needs and feel valued, they ran around, often with a constant smile on their face, attempting to please one or both parents.

People-pleasing is often confused with being kind and selfless. If anyone, including the please-pleaser, questions why they can never seem to say the word "no," they will respond with something like, "I'm just trying to be nice," or "I can't let them down."

People-pleaser craves to feel needed and indispensable because they do not value themselves. As a result, they are constantly seeking external validation.

It works to some extent. However, it is a long way from what they truly require, which is to know self-love and self-worth.

As a result, they frequently allow others to take advantage of them. As a result, it's not uncommon for a people-pleaser to find themselves in an abusive relationship, with the abusive partner constantly taking from them and the people-pleasing partner constantly giving all of themselves and attention all of the time.

People-pleasing and codependency

A healthy relationship involves an equal amount of give and take from both partners. It's also why the majority of codependents are people-pleasers, though not all people-pleasers are codependent.

Being a people-pleaser is a stressful and often painful way to live. Because no matter how much they give to others, they never receive what they truly desire. The true answer comes from within.

As a result, people-pleasers are prone to depression, stress, and anxiety. They will keep emotions bottled up, such as what they truly want to say to someone who is always taking from them.

Then there could be addiction issues as they try to suppress negative feelings of frustration and anger, some of which are directed at themselves for never being able to say no. They rarely have "me" time or any spare time because they are constantly doing things for other people.

Major indicators of people-pleasing:

- ★ *Saying yes when you really mean no*
- ★ *Cannot handle anger*
- ★ *Feeling in command of another person's emotional state*
- ★ *Conflict avoidance*
- ★ *They never express negative emotions.*
- ★ *You don't have time for yourself.*
- ★ *Imitation of those around me*
- ★ *Seeking attention at all costs*
- ★ *Constantly apologizing*
- ★ *Even when you disagree with someone, you can still agree with them.*

Chapter 2

Reasons

People, especially around the holidays, feel compelled to give everything they have to others. Whether it's listening to friends who are in need, giving gifts, or going above and beyond for others. You may be a people-pleaser if you find yourself doing this to the point of exhaustion. This usually means that you prioritize the needs of those around you over your own. The following are some of the reasons you may identify as a people pleaser:

Concerned About Rejection
Most people are afraid of being rejected. It could be a fear of being rejected from a job or by another person. If you are afraid of being rejected, you will try to avoid it at all costs. For example, if you are concerned that you will be rejected by your boss and fired one day, you may go out of your way to please your boss regardless of the cost to your mental health. Another example is that if you are afraid that your partner will leave you, you will work harder to please them rather than expecting the same in return.

Afraid Of Disappointing Others
Nobody wants to hear that they are a letdown to others. However, we cannot please everyone. There are a few people who will be impossible to please. We are not all perfect, and you will almost certainly be disappointed by another person you meet in your life. If you try to please everyone, your mental health will suffer as a result.

Desire To Avoid Conflict
It is usually easier to agree with what others say. You may find yourself avoiding confrontations with others in order to make them happy, or you may find yourself agreeing with what they say despite your feelings. While conflict has a negative connotation, it is a necessary part of communication and helps us grow. If you can resolve a disagreement with another person at work, school, or elsewhere, you will become a stronger and better person. If you avoid conflict by appeasing everyone, you will most likely accumulate a great deal of resentment.

Want Something In Exchange
You may go above and beyond for your friends and family in the hopes of receiving the same level of care and attention in return. However, not

everyone is capable of giving as much time, attention, gifts, or love as another.

This would make you believe that you are devoting far more energy and effort to your relationships than others. You may believe that no one cares about you as much as you do about them. However, this is not always the case. It's possible that the other people in your life practice self-care, in which they devote time, energy, or money to taking care of themselves first. It is critical for everyone to strike a healthy balance between self-care and being present for others.

Wish For Others To Be Nice

You believe that if you are nice to others, everyone will be nice to you. Regrettably, this is not always the case. For example, suppose you're checking out at Target and you go out of your way to be nice to the cashier by asking how their day has gone. This worker may react negatively or refuse to acknowledge your kindness. You may be offended because you went out of your way to be nice to a stranger and expect the same courtesy in return. However, it is possible that the customer before you just yelled at this cashier, or that this cashier has just received devastating personal news. You never know what other people thinking or going through. Even if you are nice to someone, it does not guarantee that they will reciprocate your kindness.

Desire To Fit In

It's possible that you want a certain group of people to like you and accept you into their circle. You may go out of your way to conform to their expectations. Assume you're a high school student looking to make friends with a particular group. You are likely to be willing to do things for them that you would not do otherwise. To fit in with them, you may go out of your way to do their homework, dress like them, or make fun of another student. This is fairly common among people-pleasers who want to fit in.

Others Can Easily Influence You

Some people are easily persuaded to believe and feel certain things. If you follow a popular icon on social media, you might be tempted to buy their wares if they look appealing. If there is a current trend to wear scrunchies, you will most likely succumb to the trend and begin wearing scrunchies. If others tell you what to do, you will most likely listen and obey without question.

Genuinely Concerned

This is the most common reason for wanting to please others. It's wonderful to be a genuine person with a lot of empathy for others. It means you genuinely care about everyone around you. If you fall into this category, you will usually discover that you are not taking care of yourself. You get so caught up in taking care of everyone else that you forget about your own self-care, which is pushed to the bottom of your to-do list.

Don't Want To Feel Responsible For Saying No

Saying "no" is extremely difficult for people-pleasers. You struggle with setting boundaries and knowing your limits. You are so concerned with pleasing others that you will say "yes" to everything anyone asks you without hesitation. It is critical for everyone to understand their own limits and to know when to say "no."

External Validation is The Source Of Your Self-worth

In the age of social media and likes, you may find yourself needing others to validate whether or not you are a good person. Perhaps you go out of your way to pay for a stranger's Starbucks order, which is very nice. But then you feel compelled to share it on Facebook so that others can validate your character. Or you post a photo of yourself in a new outfit, only to discover that your followers don't think it suits you. Then you return your new outfit. Examples like these demonstrate that you are easily influenced by what others think of you rather than how you feel about yourself.

Do not Love Yourself

For people-pleasers, this is the most overlooked part. They are always willing to help or be there for others. When it comes down to it, however, they are only there for themselves. People-pleasers are typically excellent listeners and provide the best advice. But they are unable to follow their own advice. People-pleasers rarely feel good or worthy enough to help themselves.

Chapter 3

The Root Causes

The root cause of people pleasing varies from person to person, and there are frequently additional reasons for the behavior. Although there are several causes for the ongoing desire to please others, the most common is a lack of self-confidence.

People Pleasing is a reaction to trauma and/or stress that can become one of the primary ways a person deals with difficulties. People-pleasing may appear to be who you are, but it is actually something you learned to do.

This is because we are hardwired to protect ourselves in various ways. Pleasing is now recognized as one of four trauma responses (the other three being fight, flight, and fawn). People pleasers seek safety by blending with others' desires, needs, and demands.

Because pleasing is an automatic response, this protective strategy begins mostly outside of our conscious awareness. It either becomes one of our go-to strategies for automatically protecting ourselves when we feel emotionally or relationally unsafe over time. Or we develop some flexibility and the ability to respond in a variety of ways.

It stands to reason that one of the automatic reactions is to please or agree with whoever you feel threatened by, at least until you can get some space from this person. However, if this becomes your default mode for almost everything, your happiness, physical well-being, and relationship satisfaction will suffer over time.

Pleasing can be an especially difficult reaction to change because it is frequently socially and culturally reinforced in families, the workplace, and educational systems. What begins as you attempting to please others, keep the peace, or gain the approval of others is usually encouraged and conditioned as the right and best thing to do.

Once you recognize that this is limiting your happiness and personal growth, you can take the necessary steps to boost your self-esteem. Even though every person is unique, there are some common triggers. *Some of the most common root causes of people pleasing are:*

Childhood memories

Many people who struggle with people pleasing tendencies may have been subjected to a traumatic event, neglect, or abuse as children, which led them to believe that their needs and desires were unimportant. As a result, in order to feel safe and valued, they may have learned to prioritize the needs of others over their own.

Formal social conditioning

Society frequently reinforces the notion that being kind and accommodating to others is virtuous, particularly for women. Being assertive or putting oneself first is perceived as selfish or rude. This message is especially powerful for women, who are frequently socialized to prioritize the needs of others over their own. As a result, many women believe that they don't matter and that their entire focus should be on taking care of others.

Fear of being rejected or abandoned

People pleasers may be motivated by a fear of rejection or abandonment, and they may believe that their personal worth is determined by their ability to please others. Childhood experiences, relationships, and other life events can all contribute to the reinforcement of this belief.

Self-esteem issues

People who have low self-esteem may feel compelled to constantly please others in order to gain their approval and feel valuable. They may believe that their own needs and desires are unimportant and that in order to be accepted, they must always put others first.

It is critical to recognize that the source of people pleasing is complex and multifaceted, and that each individual's experience is unique. However, by investigating the underlying beliefs and experiences that motivate people pleasing behavior, you can gain a better understanding of yourself and work toward positive change.

It is critical to understand that you were not born this way. God did not create you to please others, but to please Himself. He also does not want you to belittle yourself. He loves you and wants you to love and respect yourself. When you have a people-pleasing personality, you lose sight of how God created you, which is unique, perfect, worthy, and capable.

Chapter 4

The Effect on Happiness

What's the big deal about pleasing others? Isn't it nice and respectable to assist others and strive to make them happy? The problem with being a people-pleaser is that it extends far beyond kindness and involves changing your own habits and demands to accommodate the habits and demands of others.

With the above explanation, it's easy to see how people-pleasing can be detrimental to one's health and wellness, as pleasers can potentially harm themselves, their career, their health, and their relationships in order to give people what they want. How does pleasing others actually harm your health and happiness, and how can you start putting yourself first? Let us investigate together:

Depression and stress
People-pleasing frequently leads to repressed emotions. If you do this for an extended period of time, it can lead to frustration, anxiety, low self-esteem, and even depression. Aside from negatively impacting your psychological well-being, stress and depression can have physical consequences such as sleep problems, exhaustion, a slower immune response, and weight problems.

People-pleasers can do the opposite by attempting to please everyone around them and setting a good example for their children and family. People can prioritize their own time instead of constantly trying to help others and solve their problems for them. Spend quality time with your loved ones, share activities and chores, and set aside some "me-time" to teach others valuable life skills and demonstrate how to properly respect you.

Self-neglect
People-pleasers devote the majority of their time and energy to helping others, which can be time and energy-consuming, leaving no time to exercise, eat properly, or devote time to relaxation and hobbies. To be a good worker, a good parent, a good son or daughter, and a good partner to your spouse, you must first fuel your own body and mind.

To nurture others, you must have energy and emotional stability, which cannot be obtained through self-neglect. And don't mistake thinking about your own needs and desires for selfishness; it's actually healthy and beneficial for everyone around you. Self-care and self-love include relaxing and pampering, as well as meeting other needs such as expressing your opinions, taking time to sort out your emotions, and voicing your needs in various relationships in your life.

When it comes to self-neglect, women are the most vulnerable. Women frequently prevent their own ability to thrive by remaining in toxic relationships and always putting their family's needs ahead of their own. This is especially true for menopausal women, who may be experiencing hormonal and physical changes in addition to the stress. And nowadays, it's simple to find proper menopause treatment that can alleviate symptoms and make the transition easier and smoother. Self-care entails seeking assistance when needed in all aspects and stages of life, particularly when it comes to health and well-being.

Resentment and rage

Repressing your own thoughts and feelings in order to give others what they want to hear can lead to a buildup of anger and resentment that can explode. People-pleasing often results in more selfishness and manipulation rather than the spreading of love, help, and generosity that the pleaser might expect.

Kindness is a wonderful thing that benefits everyone, but it must come from a good place. Kindness must be given without the desire to gain approval or for any other selfish reason. When you feel the need to assist someone, consider why you want to assist them. Is it to spread happiness and make someone's life better? Will you feel cheated if your actions do not produce the desired results?

Physical Changes

People require free time to exercise, pursue hobbies, prepare nutritious meals, shop, have fun, and so on. When there isn't time for these self-care activities, it can lead to overeating or undereating, substance abuse, exhaustion, fatigue, lack of sleep, and a slew of other physical problems. Instead of always putting others first, put yourself first, and you'll be much happier, even if you start looking for validation in all the wrong places.

Chapter 5

Setting Boundaries

Boundaries are an important part of self-care. They are normal, healthy, and necessary. I still have the journal entry that sparked my interest in setting boundaries.

A stranger had engaged me in aggressive conversation for thirty minutes, sprinkled with flirtation, and slipped his bony hand around my waist. I'd fake-smiled my way through his behavior before fleeing to the bathroom.

As is often the case, I was unable to speak up for myself. I'd waited in silence, hoping the man would sense my distress and give me some space. The next morning, I took up my pen and wrote about setting boundaries, communicating authentically, and listening to my inner self.

This challenge appears in all aspects of my life. My tendency to please others created an imbalance in my relationships with friends, lovers, and coworkers. It could be as simple as staying too long in a boring conversation or offering to help a friend when I didn't have the time. It got to the point where I would sleep with someone I didn't want to sleep with because I didn't want to "hurt his feelings."

I was constantly betraying myself, designing my life around the desires of others. As a result, my life felt mediocre, underwhelming, and unidentifiable.

Women are taught from a young age to be people-pleasers, accommodating, and self-sacrificing. Under the weight of our commitments, imbalanced relationships, and carefully constructed personas, we can lose touch with our authentic, empowered selves over time.

Everything changed when I went through a difficult breakup and realized I'd always been solely responsible for my own happiness.

I realized this was my opportunity to cultivate a nurturing, supportive relationship with my inner self: the woman beneath the acting and people-pleasing. For the first time, I resolved to prioritize myself, set firm boundaries, and communicate authentically with others.

If you leave conflicts wishing you'd spoken up for yourself; if you feel drained in social situations because you feel like you're performing; if you over-commit to obligations while under-commit, if you engage in activities that bring you joy; if you agree to be intimate with people but later come to regret your decision; if you feel that you give a lot more than you receive in your relationships: this could be the year you break the pattern and start speaking and living your truth.

Here are some pointers to help you turn your boundary-setting journey into simple, actionable habits.

Practice saying "no thanks" without providing an explanation
It's natural to feel the need to justify your boundaries to others. But you don't, and sometimes the most straightforward, honest response is "No, thanks." Making an excuse or fabricating your reasoning can leave you feeling guilty or out of sync with your inner self.

Experiment with saying "No, thanks" and nothing else. Begin by saying "No, thanks" when your housemate asks if you want to watch a TV show or "No, thanks" when someone offers you a drink at the bar.

Remove yourself from a toxic friendship
Perhaps you have a friend who constantly relies on you as a sounding board for his or her problems, or who asks for favors but never returns them. Perhaps you have a friend whose personal difficulties are interfering with your own sense of well-being.

Taking a break from relationships that no longer serve you is one of the most difficult, yet rewarding forms of boundary setting.

If you have a one-sided friendship that makes you feel invisible, unheard, or disrespected, resolve to end the relationship. Remember, prioritizing your own well-being is not selfish or cruel. Healthy friendships are mutually nourishing and reciprocal, rather than one-sided and depleting.

Create a post-boundary mantra
Setting boundaries will be a major adjustment to old patterns if you have a history of people-pleasing, complete with the expected growing pains. As a result, feeling guilty, selfish, or embarrassed after setting a (completely valid) boundary is completely normal.

Be patient with yourself and recognize that developing your boundary-setting muscle takes time. Meanwhile, create a mantra to refer to after establishing difficult boundaries with others. "It is an act of self-love to set boundaries," or "I set boundaries to feel safe."

Your mantra can serve as an anchor, a constant reminder that this difficult journey is in your best interests.

Choose a cheerleader
I benefited greatly from sharing my successes with a best friend who encouraged me every step of the way during my boundary-setting process. She witnessed my journey and assisted me in recognizing my progress when I was feeling self-critical.

Designate a trusted friend, family member, or partner to be your boundary cheerleader. Explain your desire for a supportive buddy throughout the process and your intention to set better boundaries. When you establish a new boundary, notify your cheerleader and carve out space for the two of you to celebrate your success—in person, over the phone, or with a high-five emoji.

Consider how your life will be different as a result
Instead of focusing on oversharing and people-pleasing, consider the numerous benefits of setting boundaries. Allow yourself to imagine how your life will change once you start speaking your truth. How will you alter your behavior? How will your daily life be improved? How can you feel more genuine in your relationships? Keep your vision in mind as you make the best decisions for yourself on a daily basis.

In interactions with others, express your emotions
Overwhelming, anger, and frustration can be useful guideposts as you figure out when, where, and with whom to set boundaries. These feelings indicate that others may be invading your personal time or space. Developing emotional literacy allows you to set effective boundaries in the future. Instead of ignoring your emotions, ask yourself, "What am I feeling? What is causing this reaction in me? What would have to change for me to feel more secure?"

Prepare your disclaimer for your well-being
To set the tone for a compassionate, permissive discussion, begin conversations about boundaries with a disclaimer. This can be a particularly useful tool if you're afraid of upsetting existing long-term relationships with family or lovers by changing entrenched patterns.

Break the ice by sharing your intention to establish boundaries. Explain why it's important to you and how you think it'll help you. Focusing on your own well-being initiates a meaningful exchange centered on an undeniable value: your own wellness and health.

Thank others for establishing boundaries
People who have difficulty setting boundaries often have difficulty responding to boundaries set by others. Prior to learning to set my own boundaries, I frequently felt dismissed, angry, or rejected when friends or lovers imposed limits on our interactions. As I realized that people set boundaries to protect their own well-being, I purposefully cultivated a grateful attitude by responding to others with "I value your honesty" or "I appreciate you sharing that with me"—even if the boundary was difficult to hear. These friends and lovers became my role models, showing me what a life with healthy boundaries could be like.

Boundaries are tools for feeling safe, strong, and empowered in our relationships. As your journey progresses, you'll begin to feel more empowered by the realization that it's not only your right but also your duty to make the best choices for yourself.

Chapter 6

Developing Self-Esteem

While the meaning of many "self" phrases, such as self-worth, self-esteem, self-confidence, and so on, is debatable and can be interchangeable, in my opinion, self-worth is a deep self of being "enough". It refers to a sense of being loved, good enough, worthy, and valuable for who you are.

As a result, a person who lacks sufficient self-worth will almost always look to the outside for signs that they are worthy, requiring constant external validation and reassurances that they are loved.

Saying no can be frightening because feeling loved and worthy is dependent on the approval of others, which we fear we will lose if we don't make everyone happy all of the time.

However, it has the potential to go even further. The desire to gain approval from others can indicate that a person is so determined to fit in that they loses touch with who they are. They're so used to tuning into the needs of others that they can't tune into their own. This can include being aware of their preferences for spending their time, their interests and hobbies, and whether they are sleepy, hungry, angry, or depressed. People's pleasing behavior may be due to a lack of understanding rather than a fear of saying no.

It is also common for someone to have a strong sense of motivation to achieve specific objectives because they feel that doing so will enhance their value and gain acceptance from others. For example "I am only competent if I do well at work," or "I am only good enough if I have enough close associates." While a person may feel well if these parameters are met, it all comes apart if they are not. As a result, they are constantly striving to meet what they perceive to be external expectations, which adds to their stress.

The problem is that seeking validation from others will never result in the feeling of being loved that a people pleaser seeks, because it is always fleeting.

As a result, while there are many effective tools for people pleasing, such as challenging thoughts and setting boundaries, I believe that a person will always need to people please when the opinion of others is more important than their own.

Causes of Low Self-Worth

Most people who lack self-esteem have had certain childhood experiences that have shaped how they view themselves. As an example:

- ★ *Parents who were emotionally and/or physically neglectful, as well as drug addicts.*
- ★ *Being a victim of school bullying*
- ★ *Absent parents as a result of divorce or death.*
- ★ *Sibling rivalry or a competitive environment.*
- ★ *As a child, I felt responsible for an adult and a sibling.*
- ★ *Having critical or demanding parents makes it difficult to feel good enough.*
- ★ *Children were afraid of their parents' reactions because they were unable to control their own moods.*
- ★ *Physically, mentally, and emotionally abusive parents*

Being loved and accepted by our primary caregivers helped us survive in terms of evolution. We don't feel safe unless we constantly seek and gain the approval of those around us if we don't feel loved enough.

It's understandable for a child to grow up feeling unlovable if he or she has been physically, verbally, or emotionally abused. Even loving but demanding and/or emotionally distant parents can send the message that a child is only worthy of love and attention if they achieve certain goals.

How to boost your self-esteem and stop pleasing others

Improving self-worth is a long process, and working with a therapist may be beneficial, especially if you had a traumatic and/or abusive childhood. However, you can begin to work on this yourself by using evidence-based self-help tools, such as the ones listed below:

Recognition
The first step is to recognize that your people-pleasing behavior stems from a desire to gain validation and love from others that you do not have for yourself.

Mindfulness

This allows you to become more aware of, and step back from, unhelpful thoughts and feelings that fuel low self-esteem and people-pleasing. Furthermore, it can heighten your awareness of your feelings in the present moment, implying that you are more tuned in to them.

Compassion for Oneself

This is a powerful tool that works in tandem with mindfulness to help you recognize shame and self-criticism patterns and develop a kinder, more accepting relationship with yourself.

Meditations on Loving Kindness

These are specifically designed to assist you in cultivating a sense of well-wishing towards yourself, thereby increasing self-worth and self-love.

Thoughts that are difficult to accept

Examine your assumptions about your own self-worth, such as "I have to be perfect to be loved." Consider whether you would expect the same from other people you care about.

Behavioral Experiments

Consider what you would do if you didn't care what other people thought or if you already felt good enough. Examine how you feel about yourself and your relationships afterward. This can aid in the gradual transition to empowerment.

Affirmations

In moments of self-doubt, saying phrases you know you need to hear can help. "I am good enough as I am," "I love and accept myself exactly as I am," or writing positive loving letters to yourself are some examples.

Chapter 7

Assertiveness Training

When it comes to our business and personal relationships, I believe that becoming more assertive can solve many of the problems that nice people face. Nice people are wonderful. They are endearing. They're entertaining to be around for a while and they make you feel more confident in yourself.

But simply being nice isn't enough. Because nice people lie as well. They tell you to lie about yourself because they don't want to hurt your feelings. They avoid saying things to you that they should because they don't want to upset you. Many of their decisions are motivated by self-interest. That is, their niceness is motivated more by what others think of them, specifically their desire for other people to like them, than by genuine concern, care, and interest in the other person.

There is a cost for simply being nice. The nice person leads an "unlived" existence. They don't make their own calls. Other people choose their path in life. They "accompany" the crowd. And they acquiesce to the demands and whims of others in order to "be nice."

Relationships with nice people are less intimate and satisfying than they would like. True fulfilling relationships necessitate two people who interact on deep interpersonal levels with one another. The nice person gives up everything, suppressing their own individuality in order to conform to the image that the other person demands or expects. They lose themselves, and as a result, they lose the ability to truly love. Their relationships devolve into "acquaintances" rather than long-lasting friendships.

The nice person loses the affection of those around them. When someone remains submissive in a relationship, it has a psychological effect on the other person. They start to feel guilty for always getting their way, which leads to feelings of pity, irritation, and disgust for the "nice" person.

The nice person's feelings for others tend to fade over time. The nice person develops resentment as they suppress their own feelings in order to meet the demands of others. If you start by sacrificing yourself for those you love, you will end up hating those you sacrificed yourself for.

Now, before you accuse me of using an overly broad brush, let me clarify. Not all "nice" people fit the stereotype I just created. Many nice people are genuine, caring, and genuinely interested in others. Instead of labeling these people as "nice," I should probably criticize the act of being nice.

There's a big difference between being nice for the sake of being nice (e.g., not upsetting people, not causing conflict, having people like us, etc.) and truly being good. Being nice is a quality of goodness, but it goes deeper. Being nice is a charade that pretends to be good but never reaches its depth.

When we are simply nice, we do not say the things we need to say to maintain our own security in the hope of having better relationships. For example, when someone wrongs us, we don't tell them because we want to be nice - because we want them to like us. When someone's actions (or lack thereof) begin to devastate our team, being nice can prevent us from confronting them about what they're doing, thereby exacerbating the problem.

When we are truly good, when we truly care about the other person, we have the courage to say what needs to be said. We are willing to defend ourselves when someone is causing us or our team harm. We are willing to say what needs to be said not only for ourselves but also because we genuinely care about the other person and want to help them grow beyond whatever limitation or action is holding them back. This is how becoming more assertive can benefit both us and others.

The Advantages of Being More Assertive

The issue is that nice people are nice. People who are nice enjoy being nice. Nice people frequently have difficulty saying and doing difficult things because they believe that if they do, they will no longer be nice. Assertiveness is the solution for assisting nice people in transitioning from nice to good.

Being assertive allows us to say and do things in our relationships that make them more meaningful, rich, and fulfilling, which is something that being nice does not. The best relationships are those in which we approach each other as equals, recognizing the other person's goodness and best qualities as well as their flaws and limitations. At the same time, we enter those relationships with an understanding of our own strengths and weaknesses. Working through those challenges and obstacles together strengthens our bonds. You can't do that if all you want to do is be nice all the time.

Becoming more assertive can provide us with the tools we need to walk down those roads with the other people in our lives, to say what we need to say and do what we need to do to enrich both of our lives and, perhaps, make the world a little bit better. Assertiveness enables us to be more than just nice.

The Difficulty of Developing Assertiveness

Why is becoming more assertive so difficult? Fear and a lack of knowledge, I believe, are the two primary reasons that prevent people from becoming more assertive.

People who are nice are typically nice because they are afraid of conflict and/or confrontation. They are afraid that speaking their minds will destroy some of their most important relationships. They are afraid that if they assert themselves, the other person will dislike them, become angry, and retaliate. Perhaps it is because their personality is more flight than fight. Perhaps it's cowardice. Maybe it's just not wanting the drama, and the resolution isn't worth the time and effort it would take to have a difficult conversation. It could be any of these. However, nice people will sometimes use these as justifications for their avoidance, and once you get into the habit of avoidance in your relationships, whether business or personal, it can be difficult to break.

The lack of knowledge is another reason people aren't more assertive. We have no idea how to start a difficult conversation. We don't know what to say. We don't know how to confidently express our feelings and emotions.

The good news is that addressing the second part is relatively simple. In other words, you can become more assertive by learning and implementing techniques that will enable you to speak the right words at the right time and enter a difficult conversation with confidence. The other part is more difficult because overcoming fear requires developing the courage to do what you know you must do. Gaining and improving your communication skills, on the other hand, will give you confidence, which will help you overcome fear.

Aggressiveness vs. Assertiveness

Now, a word about the distinction between assertiveness and aggression. Nice people can be dominated by aggressive people. This is evident in dysfunctional relationships. Aggressive people say whatever they want, regardless of the consequences or the relationship havoc they may cause. They only think about themselves and don't give a damn about anyone else. You might imagine aggressive people as two-year-olds throwing a temper tantrum to get what they want. Some aggressive people fit this description, but others are bullies who use intimidation to further their own goals.

Some of these people may be unaware of what they are doing and act in this manner out of habit or past conditioning. Assertiveness can help them learn to see what they are doing and how it is affecting the other people in their lives and straining their relationships in these situations. Being assertive with these people is essential if we truly care about them because it is the only way they will see the reality of their actions. Speaking the truth to them in a caring and strategic manner may be the only way for them to grow out of their intimidation tactics and become a contributing and functional member of the organization, relationship, and society in general.

Others, on the other hand, are aggressive by design and intent. They intimidate and bully others on purpose in order to dominate them and position themselves at the top of the dominance hierarchy. You might want to label these people as "evil," but who knows what motivates them to do what they do? Assertiveness is even more important in these situations because it allows you to stand up for yourself and refuse to be dominated by an aggressive person. Assertiveness empowers you to protect your own dignity and advocate for your rights. In this case, assertiveness protects and strengthens your integrity.

Developing Assertiveness

Here are some steps that can really help nice people grow and develop their assertiveness skills.

Be Brave
This characteristic is possibly the most difficult to overcome. Most nice people would say they are self-assured. Most nice people would agree that they value other people. But they're terrified. And, to be honest, difficult conversations are terrifying. As previously stated, nice people are afraid of conflict. Who knows what will happen? Or what the other person will say? Will they continue to like us? Will our friendship last? Who knows what will happen once it's all over?

Uncertainty can cause fear, which paralyzes us and keeps us from doing and saying what we need to do and say. The only way to overcome fear is through bravery. To have the heart when your heart appears to be weak. That is bravery. To enter the arena when every fiber of your being tells you not to. That is bravery. To charge into battle while arrows fly by your face and your legs refuse to move. That is bravery.

According to C.S. Lewis, courage is the virtue that puts every other virtue to the test. In other words, being virtuous necessitates a courageous step. Honesty necessitates bravery. Courage is required for integrity. Character necessitates bravery. In this case, assertiveness necessitates bravery.

Improve Your Self-Confidence
One of the constraints that nice people face that prevents them from becoming more assertive is a lack of self-confidence. We are unable to be assertive because we have low self-esteem and self-worth.

We don't want people to dislike us because of our insecurities. So, if we base our self-worth on what others think of us, we are allowing them to define our existence. When we are enslaved to the opinions of others, we are prevented from experiencing what philosophers call "our authentic mode of existence." We aren't being honest with ourselves.

To move beyond being bound by the opinions of others, we must have the courage to question reality. You need to evaluate your own self-worth and how much you rely on the opinions of others. Only when we recognize a weakness can we begin to work on improving our own self-esteem.

When you have a higher sense of self-esteem and self-worth, the opinions of others don't matter as much. When you have more confidence in yourself, you can act, say, and do whatever needs to be done without worrying about what others will think.

Consider the Other Person
Another reason we may not say or do what we should is that we do not care about the other person. Consider this. If you truly care about someone, you would or should tell them if they do something that is harmful to their health. We often hear the cliche that "real" friends tell the truth and will call you out when you need it. Unfortunately, many people either do not have "real" friends or do not care about them.

When you truly value someone, you prioritize them over their short-term perception of you. When you truly care about someone, you are more concerned with their life and future than with whether their feelings will be hurt or if they will dislike you because you tell them the truth about themselves. Genuinely valuing someone entails putting their best interests and future ahead of their immediate feelings or discomfort.

Put yourself in their shoes as well. If you were destroying yourself the way they are, wouldn't you want your friends to be honest with you even if it meant making you angry or offended? The majority of us would say yes. Most of us want our friends to speak the truth in love about important issues.

Of course, some people would prefer to live a lie. Some people would rather not know the truth about themselves because it would necessitate introspection, action, and possibly even a major life transformation. Many people prefer to live in denial. That is regrettable.

However, the fact remains that truly valuing someone else - truly caring about their life and future - is a prerequisite for assertiveness. That doesn't mean you have to say what needs to be said, but if you don't truly value the other person, you won't say or do what needs to be said or done.

Assertiveness Techniques

Learning techniques that make assertiveness easier is one way to help you overcome the fear that often prevents assertiveness. Here are three suggestions:

Address the behavior rather than the person
Phrasing your conversation around the other person's specific actions also helps to avoid defensiveness. Again, if the other person becomes defensive, the conversation can quickly derail. When you address the fault in the behavior rather than the person's character, it may be easier for them to see the error of their ways.

Learn how to personalize
Personalizing your communication means framing it from your own point of view rather than attributing it to someone else. This entails speaking in an "I" voice. So, instead of saying, "You're a jerk!" you say, "I feel disrespected when you act like that."

The words we use and the manner in which we use them have an emotional impact. Words with a "you" perspective for example, "you always" or "you never," are like a big finger pointing right into someone's face. These phrases immediately raise emotional barriers and cause the other person to become defensive. When this happens, it's no longer about the issue; it's about preserving one's ego.

Consider it from a different angle
When people tell us how bad we are, we can easily become defensive, angry, and resentful. They are slandering our reputation!! However, if someone says that our behavior in a specific instance was inappropriate, the emotional impact is reduced because, after all, we can adjust our behavior. We have a more difficult time changing who we are as individuals.

Use the template for assertive messages. These techniques can be combined to create an assertive message template. This is how it works:

Describe a Particular Behaviour
The first part of the three-part assertive message describes a specific behavior. You begin by saying, "When you do ___________," followed by the specific behavior you wish to confront. Again, you should address the behavior in a nonjudgmental manner. Defensiveness can result from general descriptions, assigning motives, or judging the other person. Make it specific and about the behavior itself, without passing judgment.

Personalize Your Emotions
Following the description of the specific behavior, you would say something like "I feel____________." This personalization - putting things in "I" terms - lets the other person know how you feel about their behavior in a non-threatening or non-judgmental way. Your emotions are valid, and it is critical that you express them. In this case, you should use a specific word that accurately describes how you feel. This can be difficult at times because we don't always know how to express and/or define our emotions, or we don't have the right words to say. Learning how to accurately describe your feelings, on the other hand, can help the other person understand how they are contributing to the problem.

Give a Specific Outcome
Finally, describe a specific outcome of the other person's behavior. Inform them of how their actions affect your performance. Ascertain that the concrete outcome is not judgmental or assigns motives to their behavior. Perhaps it is inconvenient for you. Perhaps it's forcing you to pick up their load. Whatever it

is, make sure you tell them so they understand how their behavior is affecting you. They might not have considered it.

Allow them to Respond
After conveying an assertive message to someone, remain silent and wait for them to respond. This allows them to accept responsibility for their actions and begin a dialogue that will hopefully lead to a solution. If nothing else, it can serve as a foundation for addressing the issue again if it persists.

We're all trying to be nice. It is preferable to be excellent. Assertiveness can bridge the gap between niceness and assertiveness. Self-confidence can be increased through assertiveness. It can assist you in demonstrating how much you value and care about other people. And it can give you great opportunities to strengthen your courage when you face scary situations in life. Assertiveness is the skill that can transform "nice" people into truly great people.

Chapter 8

Overcoming Rejection Fear

Fear of rejection is a strong emotion that can have far-reaching consequences in our lives. Most people get nervous when they put themselves in situations where they might be rejected, but for some, the fear becomes overwhelming.

Many factors can contribute to this fear. Untreated rejection anxiety can worsen over time, causing a person's life to become increasingly limited.

Psychological Results

Fear of rejection causes us to act in ways that make us appear insecure, ineffective, and overwhelmed. You may sweat, shake, fidget, avoid eye contact, and even lose your ability to communicate effectively. While people react to these behaviors in a variety of ways, these are some of the reactions you might see.

Ironically, rejection anxiety frequently becomes a self-fulfilling prophecy. It is common knowledge in popular psychology that confidence boosts attractiveness. In general, the lack of self-confidence that comes with rejection anxiety makes us more likely to be rejected.

According to research, confidence is almost as important as intelligence in determining our income level.

Some people prey on other people's insecurities. Those who are afraid of rejection may be more vulnerable to being manipulated for someone else's personal gain.

Expert manipulators generally come across as charming, suave, and caring—they know which buttons to press in order to gain others' trust. They also know how to keep someone who is afraid of rejection on edge, as if the manipulator could leave at any time. Almost always, the manipulator leaves once they have gotten what they want from the other person.

The majority of people are decent, honest, and forthright. They will try to help rather than manipulate someone who is afraid of rejection. Look for

indications that your friends and family are encouraging your assertiveness
by asking you to be more open with them or probing your true feelings.

What It Does to Your Behavior

When you are afraid of being rejected, you may engage in behaviors that are
aimed at either covering up or compensating for your fear.

Absence of Authenticity
Many people who are afraid of rejection develop a highly controlled and
scripted lifestyle. You may live your life behind a mask if you are afraid of
being rejected if you reveal your true self to the world. This can make you
appear phony and inauthentic to others, and it can lead to a rigid refusal to
accept life's challenges.

Passivity
People who are afraid of rejection will often go to great lengths to avoid
confrontation. You may refuse to ask for what you desire or speak up for what
you require. A common tendency is to simply ignore your own needs or
pretend that they don't exist.

Fear of rejection may prevent you from realizing your full potential. Putting
yourself out there is scary for anyone, but if you are afraid of being rejected,
you may feel paralyzed. Even if you are unhappy with your current situation,
holding on to the status quo feels safe.

Passive-Aggressiveness
Many people who fear rejection end up behaving in passive-aggressive ways
because they are uncomfortable showing off their true selves but are unable
to completely shut out their own needs. You may procrastinate, "forget" to
keep promises, complain, and work inefficiently on projects.

Fear of rejection may lead to behaviors such as passive-aggressiveness,
passivity, and people-pleasing. It may additionally compromise your
authenticity and make it difficult to be yourself in public.

Where It May Have an Impact on Your Life

Although not everyone experiences rejection in the same way, it does have an impact on one's ability to succeed in a variety of personal and professional situations.

Interviews for Jobs
Fear of rejection can cause physical symptoms that are misconstrued as a lack of confidence. Many positions require confidence and an air of authority, and those who are afraid come across as weak and insecure. If you are afraid of rejection, you may have difficulty negotiating work-related contracts, resulting in lost pay and benefits.

Transactions in Business
In many jobs, the need to impress does not end when you get the job. Many jobs require you to entertain clients, negotiate deals, sell products, and attract investors. Even simple tasks like answering the phone can be terrifying for people who are afraid of rejection.

Getting to Know New People
Humans are social creatures, and we are expected to behave properly in public. If you are afraid of rejection, you may find it difficult to converse with strangers or even friends of friends. Your tendency to isolate yourself may prevent you from making long-term connections with others.

Dating
First dates can be stressful, especially for those who are afraid of being rejected. Rather than focusing on getting to know the other person and deciding whether or not you want to go on another date, you might spend all of your time worrying about whether or not that person likes you. Common symptoms include difficulty speaking, obsessive worrying about your appearance, inability to eat, and a visibly nervous demeanor.

Relationships between peers
People often behave in ways that help them fit in with the group because the desire to belong is a basic human condition. While dressing, speaking, and behaving as a group member is not always unhealthy, peer pressure can be excessive. It may lead you to do things you don't want to do just to be a part of the group.

Fear of rejection can impact many aspects of your life, including your professional success and relationships with friends and romantic partners.

How to Overcome Rejection Fear

There are steps you can take if you are afraid of rejection to learn how to cope better and stop this fear from negatively impacting your life. The following strategies may be useful in learning how to overcome a fear of rejection.

Improve Your Self-Control Skills

Self-regulation is the ability to recognize and control one's emotions and behaviors. It is also helpful in overcoming your fear of rejection.1 You can actively take steps to reframe your thinking in a more optimistic and encouraging manner by identifying negative thoughts that contribute to feelings of fear.

Confront Your Fears

Avoidance coping involves dealing with unpleasant feelings by simply avoiding the things that cause them. The issue with this approach is that it eventually leads to increased feelings of fear. Instead of helping you overcome your fear of rejection, it makes you more fearful and sensitive to it.

Instead of avoiding situations where you might face rejection, concentrate on putting yourself out there and confronting your fear. As you gain more experience confronting your fear, you'll notice that the consequences are less stressful than you anticipated. You'll also gain more faith in your own ability to succeed.

Develop Resilience

Being resilient means being able to get back up after a setback and move forward with renewed strength and optimism. Building your confidence in your own abilities, having a strong social support system, and nurturing and caring for yourself are all strategies that can help foster a greater sense of resilience. Having goals and working to improve your skills can help you believe in your ability to recover from rejection.

Taking steps to overcome your fear of rejection can help you reduce the negative impact it has on your life. Learning how to manage your emotions, confronting your fears, and cultivating a strong sense of resilience can all help you overcome your fear of rejection.

People who are afraid of rejection, on the other hand, frequently perceive these efforts as emotionally threatening. This often causes friends and family to tread carefully, afraid of exacerbating your anxieties. They may become frustrated and angry over time, either confronting you about your behavior or starting to distance themselves from you.

Chapter 9

Developing Genuine Relationships

Mental health requires authentic relationships, and close, supportive, and nurturing connections. According to research, the quality of our relationships is directly related to our happiness, well-being, and self-esteem.

Unfortunately, early childhood trauma can make it difficult to form and sustain healthy, authentic relationships. When the parent-child bond is broken early in life, the psychological scars follow us into adulthood.

Relational therapy for trauma, on the other hand, can assist young adults in healing from these experiences, understanding the characteristics of a healthy relationship, and learning how to build authentic connections. Compassion, forgiveness, and acceptance must be practiced for both others and oneself during the healing process.

When we reveal our true selves to another person, we begin to form authentic relationships. That requires us to be authentic and vulnerable in our communication and interactions. Furthermore, we are congruent, which means that what we feel on the inside is consistent with how we act and what we say to others.

When we reveal our true selves to another person, we begin to form authentic relationships. That requires us to be authentic and vulnerable in our communication and interactions.

It is not always easy to maintain genuine relationships. While we cannot control the actions of others, we can control how we respond when we are triggered. Skills for managing emotional reactivity are essential when feeling defensive, hurt, or abandoned. For example, you could take a step back and consider whether your reaction is truly motivated by the other person's actions or by your own fears and issues. Furthermore, relational therapy for trauma can assist young adults in determining whether their reactions are a result of their own childhood trauma. If this is the case, being open with others and sharing one's own story can help strengthen authentic relationships and reveal more of one's true self.

Furthermore, one of the characteristics of authentic relationships is transparency. When having an emotional conversation, for example, it is critical to be clear about your feelings so that you leave the interaction without resentment. That means being open and honest about your emotions while remaining respectful. Furthermore, active listening is a component of developing authentic connections, as it demonstrates that you are truly hearing what the other person has to say and that you value your relationship with them.

Genuine Connections and Attachment Style

The nature of a child's initial attachment bond with their parents or primary caregivers is critical. This is because the original bond determines how easily that person will be able to form authentic relationships as a young adult.

John Bowlby, a British psychoanalyst, developed attachment theory. Many of Bowlby's ideas were expanded upon by the American developmental psychologist Mary S. Ainsworth. She investigated how young children reacted when separated from their parents. She also examined how they reacted when their parents returned. As a result, she used this research to classify children into one of four attachment styles:

- ➤ *Secure*
- ➤ *Insecure and worried*
- ➤ *Insecure avoidant*
- ➤ *Insecure and disorganized*

These four attachment styles follow children into adulthood and influence their friendships, romantic relationships, family relationships, and professional relationships. As a result, children who have a secure attachment to their parents grow into adults who can trust others and form intimate relationships. Children with insecure attachment styles may grow into adults who struggle to form authentic relationships.

Attachment, Trauma, and Intimate Relationships

Trauma, attachment, and intimate relationships are all intertwined in a person's life experience, beginning in early childhood. Childhood attachment style sets the tone for future relationship patterns and interactions. In adult relationships, an insecure attachment style leads to insecurity and anxiety. Family roles formed in childhood are taken on in adulthood, according to Pia Mellody's Post Induction Therapy model for the development of immaturity and trauma resolution. In this model, three roles are represented:

Lost Child
Dependent, disempowered, passive-aggressive, manipulative, relationships "keep them alive," appears powerless, feels inferior to others

Scapegoat
Falsely empowered/disempowered, aggressive, out of control, seeks intensity to feel alive, overly dependent, and believes they are "less than"

Hero
Falsely empowered/all-powerful, passive-aggressive, manipulate others, believes they are superior to others

The client observes how their emotional reactions at the moment may be triggered by childhood traumas in relational therapy for trauma. As an example:

Wounded child
Internalizes pain and expresses it through tears/grief

Rebellious child
Internalizes resentment and expresses it through anger/rage

Adaptable and functional Adult
Presents who they want to be rather than who they are. This is not always true; they may act one way at work and another at home, for example.

Developing Genuine Relationships with Family, Friends, and Partners

Insecure attachment styles in childhood can have an impact on adult friendships, family relationships, and romantic relationships. Individuals who have insecure anxious attachment styles may be overly needy or clingy in their relationships. They may be more concerned with rejection and abandonment, as well as more jealous. As a result, they need constant reassurance from both friends and romantic partners.

Individuals who are insecure avoidant are more likely to be loners and have difficulty relying on others, whether friends or partners. They prefer to be alone and frequently believe that close relationships are more trouble than they are worth. As a form of emotional self-protection, they tend to close themselves off.

In young adulthood, the attachment style known as insecure disorganization manifests as conflicting and unresolved feelings about the past and about relationships. As a result, these people have difficulty maintaining authentic relationships and frequently cannot tolerate intimacy in relationships. Their friendships and romantic relationships may be especially volatile, with extreme highs and lows. Furthermore, people who have a disorganized attachment style are more likely to develop depression and PTSD.

Understand the Facts

Attachment styles influence family relationships even after children have matured and no longer rely on their parents.

Attachment styles influence family relationships even after children have matured and no longer rely on their parents. Indeed, research shows that an individual's attachment style formed in childhood can influence their relationship with their parents throughout adulthood.

Trauma Relational Therapy
Mental health disorders arise from underlying issues, which are frequently linked to early childhood trauma. Childhood trauma can be acute, such as the death of a parent, or it can take the form of relational trauma. Relational trauma is defined as a disruption in the child's relationship with their parent(s) or caregiver(s), which typically results in an insecure attachment style.

Furthermore, young adults who have experienced relational trauma are more likely to internalize the belief that they are not good enough or that they do not belong. This also becomes a part of who they now are. As a result, relational trauma and insecure attachment increase the likelihood of mental health issues like anxiety, depression, substance abuse, PTSD, and Obsessive Compulsive Disorder, as well as influence how we respond to stress.

Young adults' mental health typically improves when they receive therapeutic support to heal traumatic events in childhood and rediscover their true selves. As a result, there is a lower need to self-medicate through harmful behaviors like substance abuse or eating disorders.

Learning to identify the triggers for stress, fear, abandonment issues, and depressive symptoms is part of relational trauma therapy. Furthermore, relational trauma therapy may challenge core beliefs and issues in order to redefine a young adult's sense of self. Adult trauma therapy may also include multigenerational work to identify the positive and negative traits we have unconsciously inherited from our parents.

Developing the Ability to Make Genuine Connections
Fortunately, childhood trauma does not have to define and inform your relationships for the rest of your life. Furthermore, developing a secure attachment style can help heal relational trauma. This is referred to as "earned secure attachment," because adults learn to build it through conscious effort rather than instinctively through the parent-child bond. As a result of doing their own inner work to lay the groundwork, they gain skills for establishing the types of authentic relationships and authentic connections they did not have as children.

Processing childhood traumas is the first step in developing a "earned secure attachment" style. Therapy addresses the underlying issues that may be impeding the formation of genuine connections. Furthermore, young adults with insecure attachment styles learn tools for dealing with relationship stress. Furthermore, they break old behavioral patterns that have hampered their relationships in the past. As a result, they are able to strengthen existing connections while also establishing new, healthy relationships.

Developing an Earned Secure Attachment Style

Stay in the present moment
Practice mindfulness to help you stay in the present moment rather than reverting to old habits. Keep an eye on your emotions. To avoid a stress-induced reaction or trauma response, emotional awareness and regulation skills are essential.

To avoid future resentments, express feelings in the moment and in a nonreactive manner. Keep the pain from becoming internalized.

Rather than passing judgment on your own or others' actions, practice compassion, acceptance, and forgiveness. Self-compassion, in particular, is a powerful tool for fostering change and growth.

Consider your personal story
Make a coherent account of your life. Recognize your early childhood traumas. Think about how your growing understanding of the past affects your current relationships.

Look for the good in your story. Rather than blaming your parents for what you didn't get from them, concentrate on what did. Rewrite your story and list the gifts you received.

Allow yourself to feel the pain of your traumatic experiences. Grieving is part of the process of processing and healing the past. This aids in the rewiring of your brain to create a sense of security.

Make a safe attachment with someone who is emotionally open and responsive.

Building authentic connections with your therapist is the most secure place to begin.

Form genuine relationships free of emotional involvement and codependency. These can take place with coworkers or friends who are objective and present.

Once you are capable of developing secure attachments to others, start with family members, preferably parents. Allow yourself to be free of any preconceived notions about the outcome. Create the desired attachment. You are not doing this to obtain something from the other person.

Finally, the work of healing from relational trauma and developing authentic relationships, including authentic connections with oneself, can be difficult. But it's well worth it. We will never be truly happy, joyful, or free unless we have an authentic relationship with ourselves and others.

Conclusion

Make sure you're not saying 'No' to yourself when you say 'Yes' to others. What if you didn't have to recover from people-pleasing, but instead could tweak it, hone it, and turn it into your new superpower? What would that feel like?

When I read about the trait of people-pleasing, it is frequently framed negatively and as something you must recover from, much like an illness that requires treatment. It's also known as the 'disease to please,' which proves my point even more!

However, because low confidence and self-esteem are often part of the reason people struggle with this personality trait, thinking about it in these terms only exacerbates the problem and confirms your suspicions that something is wrong with you!

While overusing these traits can have negative consequences such as stress, exhaustion, anxiety, overwhelm, and burnout, to name a few, the key word here is overuse; viewing it as a shameful part of yourself that must be exercised like an evil spirit from your soul is not helpful!

There are many positive qualities of this people-pleasing part that are often overlooked when properly balanced, but as with any kind of magic, practice is required to truly master your craft and gain control of your powers.

The Dark Side of People-pleasing

The desire to please others is a coping mechanism that many people learn as children. That doesn't necessarily imply you had a bad childhood or bad parents; however, as children, we have a way of interpreting things that, if left unchallenged, can trip us up later in life.

Being the giver often feels safer than being on the receiving end. The giver has more power, while the receiver is more vulnerable. As a result, it's a way to avoid unpleasant feelings like guilt, shame, anxiety, hurt, and rejection.

If you have a strong desire to please others, you are likely to thrive on their acceptance and validation, and you will frequently abandon or dismiss your own needs in favor of theirs. You are both guilty and resentful of having to say yes.

Like a chameleon, you try to manage what others think of you by taking the temperature of the room and adjusting your behavior accordingly. And, more often than not, your self-worth is linked to your usefulness and the approval of others.

You may find yourself running around someone else's hamster wheel, exhausted, stressed, and overwhelmed, wishing for the world to come to a halt so you can get off and take a breath!

You are anxious and frustrated, and you frequently lose yourself in your desire for an easy life and not wanting to rock the boat; the reality is that life appears to be easier for everyone except you!

Many people will be unaware of your beliefs if you tend to side with the majority or sit firmly in the middle. In fact, you may have become so accustomed to conforming to others' opinions and needs while suppressing your own that you no longer know what you think or want!

It can be difficult to be completely honest with yourself and others because you are afraid of the consequences, but this does not have to be the case.

When used responsibly, people-pleasing can become your greatest superpower, propelling you to achieve your wildest dreams.

Positive Characteristics of People Pleasers

If you have people-pleasing tendencies, you are probably good at reading people and instinctively knowing how to make the best of situations. You have a natural ability to connect with others and are excellent at listening and assisting others in problem-solving.

You notice minor differences and pay attention to details, which allows you to anticipate the needs of others and make them feel seen, heard, and valued. This makes you an excellent supporter and relationship builder.

You most likely despise conflict, which means you've honed your skills at quickly defusing uncomfortable situations and devising win-win solutions.

Because you are driven to meet the needs of others and dislike disappointing them, you go above and beyond to keep your promises and are regarded as capable and dependable.

You value the happiness of those around you and will go out of your way to ensure it. However, there is a fine line between being nice, helpful, and friendly and veering into the negative aspects of this personality trait.

Any strength can become a weakness if used inappropriately or excessively. And if you have a tendency to prioritize the needs of others over your own, you must master the following skills to ensure that you use your superpowers for good rather than evil!

The Most Important Skills to Learn

Increase Your Self-Esteem and Confidence
You most likely believe your worth is determined by how useful and valuable you are to others, which puts you in a constant state of anxiety as you try to control their opinion by changing your behavior. It's not something you do consciously, but it's a draining and soul-destroying way to live.

When you begin to believe that who you are (right now) is more than enough, you can begin to detach your worth from the opinions of others. You will never be able to please everyone, no matter how hard you try, and it is not your responsibility to ensure their happiness...

The most important relationship in your life is the one you have with yourself, because you will always be with yourself, so you might as well enjoy the company.

Hold
Before you commit to assisting someone else, take a moment to check in with yourself. Does the thought of assisting this person make your heart sing or sink? Do you have the time and emotional capacity to take on this challenge? Consider whether this is something you want to do or something you feel you should do.

Determine whether you are giving from a place of love or fear
You probably do things for others at least some of the time out of a sense of duty or obligation, or out of fear of:

> *Rejection*
> *Leaving something out*
> *Conflict/Anger*
> *Being criticized/disliked*
> *Loss of control/Necessity*

Begin to ponder what motivates your desire to please. Be honest with yourself: do you have any hopes that this good deed will be returned? If so, have you informed them? Otherwise, how will the other person know?

When you give from a place of love, it feels good and there is no expectation of anything in return…

Make Peace With Uncomfortable Feelings
Because you are afraid and want to avoid unpleasant feelings like guilt and anxiety, you frequently say yes when everything inside you is screaming no. However, embracing this discomfort gives you freedom and power.

Consider your emotions and thoughts to be clouds in the sky. If you look up at the sky right now and then again in a few hours, you'll notice a difference. The sky, like our emotional well-being, is constantly changing.

Thoughts and feelings do not last. They do not form a part of you. You are the backdrop for them, just as the sky is for the clouds.

When I'm feeling down, I like to repeat to myself, 'This too shall pass.' If you do nothing else but acknowledge your feelings and sit with them for a while, they will begin to change.

Understand Boundaries
A boundary is an imaginary line that separates you and me. It depicts where you end and I begin and demonstrates how others should treat you. Consider it your house's property line. Saying no to a request when your heart sinks is an example of a boundary.

This will help you identify the areas of your life where you over-give the most and think about how you'd like it to be different — the first step in changing anything is always awareness. It will then provide you with some simple tools to experiment with in order to regain control over your life.

www.ingramcontent.com/pod-product-compliance
Lightning Source LLC
Chambersburg PA
CBHW050752250726

48662CB00005B/2176